Dedicated to Garry and Jody, who planted the seed and allowed it to grow. Your work will never be forgotten.

The Garden: A Poem of Growth

Copyright © 2022 Jordan Dale

ISBN: 9798839519848

www.monostoryacademy.com

THE GARDEN

A poem of growth

By Jordan Dale

Wholeness is psychological law.

All heroes suffer from an identity crisis. Their journey is the rediscovery of what was lost, the unification of opposites, the circling of the square, the union of the hemispheres.

This is true in story because it's true in you...

Part One

APOLLO
(Become one, not many)

"Anti-social behavior is a trait of intelligence in a world of conformists." - Nikola Tesla

The opposite of courage isn't cowardice, it's conformity.

I once had a garden that grew sovereign and free.
Walked it each day and knew the name of each tree.

All of that changed when a visitor came.
He claimed being natural brought nothing but shame.

"The problem," he said, "Is you don't know you lack.
Being wild isn't good, you've gotten off track.

Stop all this growing, come to the city with me.
I'll show you the right way to live as a tree."

So my trees left the garden to hear the wisdom of fools,
Where they learned to conform and follow the rules.

They were taught being safe always trumped being whole,
And only the ignorant believed in the soul.

Traded beauty for equality and took off their crowns.
They stopped being verbs and called themselves nouns.

Life became illusions of money and time.
Egos inflated with each counted dime.

When they were bored they all watched TV.
Programming erased their memories of me.

Engineered to stay in an alpha wave state,
They were taught to be victims and also to hate.

But one of my trees was jolted awake.
"Surely this life has to be a mistake."

Without the sun and the soil he felt hollow.
"Others will too. If I lead they will follow."

Waited all night like a solitary pawn.
But none in the city cared he was gone.

The revelation he had was only his own.
In the end he died sad, betrayed and alone.

Out of his failure a sapling grew,
Born of the parts of him that were true.

Walk in the garden again since he came.
He's given me joy and I gave him a name.

Part Two

DIONYSUS

"I'd rather be whole, than good." - Carl Jung

"I will give you treasures of darkness." - Isaiah 45:3

Ages changed and my trees came home,
Called by the one who once stood alone.

Those who sought control made him the ideal.
All of it programming to make others kneel.

Strict laws were passed to rectify fate.
They put up a wall with a sign on its gate.

Scapegoats were punished, wrongs were set right.
Those not in accord were cast into the night.

Hierarchy appeared where my garden once stood.
Participation determined if you were called good.

Experts alone became the way to salvation.
Regurgitation of facts was called education.

But one of my trees wouldn't give his consent.
He rejected their teaching and lived in the present.

Labeled a fool but too wise to be conned,
He was drawn to the wall and the mystery beyond.

So I spoke to his heart through his single eye,
"The things you can't question are always a lie."

"The sign isn't a warning, but instruction from me.
You'll have to rebel if you want to be free."

"Their orders and structure have shackled your soul.
You were born to be wild, you were born to be whole."

So he gave up all hope and found the divine.
Left the safety of their garden and walked into mine.

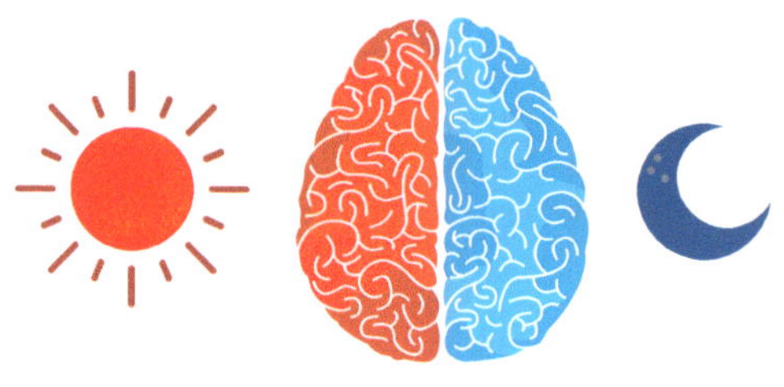

"Much will have been gained for aesthetics once we have succeeded in apprehending directly – rather than merely ascertaining – that art owes its continuous evolution to the Apollinian–Dionysian duality, even as the propagation of the species depends on the duality of the sexes, their constant conflicts and periodic acts of reconciliation. I have borrowed my adjectives from the Greeks, who developed their mystical doctrines of art through plausible embodiments, not through purely conceptual means. It is by those two art sponsoring deities Apollo and Dionysus, that we are made to recognize the tremendous split, as regards both origins and objectives, between the plastic, Apollinian arts and the nonvisual art of music inspired by Dionysus. The two creative tendencies developed alongside one another, usually in fierce opposition, each by its taunts forcing the other to more energetic production, both perpetuating in a discordant concord that agon which the term art but feebly denominates: until at last, by the thaumaturgy of an Hellenic act of will, the pair accepted the yoke of marriage and, in this condition, begot Attic tragedy, which exhibits the salient features of both parents."

from Nietzsche's The Birth of Tragedy

Author's Notes

If you are reading this then you are part of the resistance...

The Hero's Journey is the discovery that everything we know is wrong. When we fail to grasp this, we not only fail to become the hero in our own story, but we remain an NPC in someone else's. That's because we don't see the world as it is, we see it as we are. This is why all heroes take on the rebel archetype.
You see, the external journey isn't real. It's a metaphor for what happens within the mindset of the protagonist. In fact, all camera and location changes in a story are simply outer manifestations of the "journey" within as the hero rebels from the programming of the Ordinary World and reconnects with their true self. This is why all heroes start as orphans in some shape or form. It's also why there are so few heroes. The status quo depends on you not discovering this. The hardest fight you will ever face is staying yourself in a world desperate to make you like everyone else. You have no idea how important you are.
You are the <u>Noise of Knowingness</u>!!!
But like all truth, this can't be taught, only discovered. The decision, of course, is up to you. Wholeness awaits...

"To bear a ring of power is to be alone." – Galadriel
"You must unlearn all you have learned." – Yoda

Find Us At

WWW.MONOSTORYACADEMY.COM

MONOSTORYADADEMY@GMAIL.COM

Follow Us At

YOUTUBE - MONOSTORYACADEMY

TWITTER - MONOSTORY1

INSTAGRAM - MONOSTORYACADEMY

About the Author

Jordan Dale has travelled the world as a Marine, humanitarian, and an international speaker teaching story and screenwriting. He met his wife in Hawaii and his three children in North Carolina.

Be it acting, writing, filmmaking, teaching, or parenting, his message of empowerment is always the same... "There is only one story. There is only one person in that story. And that person is you."

There's only one story.
There's only one person in that story.
And that person is you.